YOU ARE AN ARTIST

Learn skills, find your style,
and build your brand!

BY AURÉLIA DURAND

DK

CONTENTS

MOTIVATION

FIRST STEPS

TAKE RISKS

EXPERIENCES

WHERE TO START?

SELF-DOUBT

SKETCHING

FAILURES

DOODLES

IDEAS

CREATIVE VISIONS

BRAINSTORMING

WORK IN PROGRESS

DISCOVERIES

RESOURCES

SUCCESS

TRAVELING

GOALS

ENTREPRENEUR

FINDING A STYLE

BECOMING

CHALLENGES

EXPERIENCES

YOU ARE AN ARTIST

INTRODUCTION

ABOUT ME

Hi everyone! Bonjour :)

I'M AURÉLIA DURAND! I live and work in a lovely part of Paris, and I'm a *PROFESSIONAL, FULL-TIME ARTIST.* I get to create art all the time, and I've worked with many famous brands, including *The New Yorker*, *Nike*, and Google. My book, *This Book Is Anti-Racist*, was even a super-popular **#1 New York Times bestseller.**

I'm what's called a "multidisciplinary artist", which means I use lots of different things to make art. I *PAINT*, do *DICITAL ART*, use *PHOTOGRAPHY*, make *ANIMATIONS*, and more. My goal is to make people happy and spread peaceful messages with my art, and I use bright colors and cool patterns to do that!

In this book, I want to show you how you can find your own artistic voice using pictures and drawings to help explain things. I also want to share my journey of becoming an artist with you. I hope that telling my story will inspire you to think about what **you** can do, too.

DEVELOP
YOUR
ARTISTRY
WITH ME

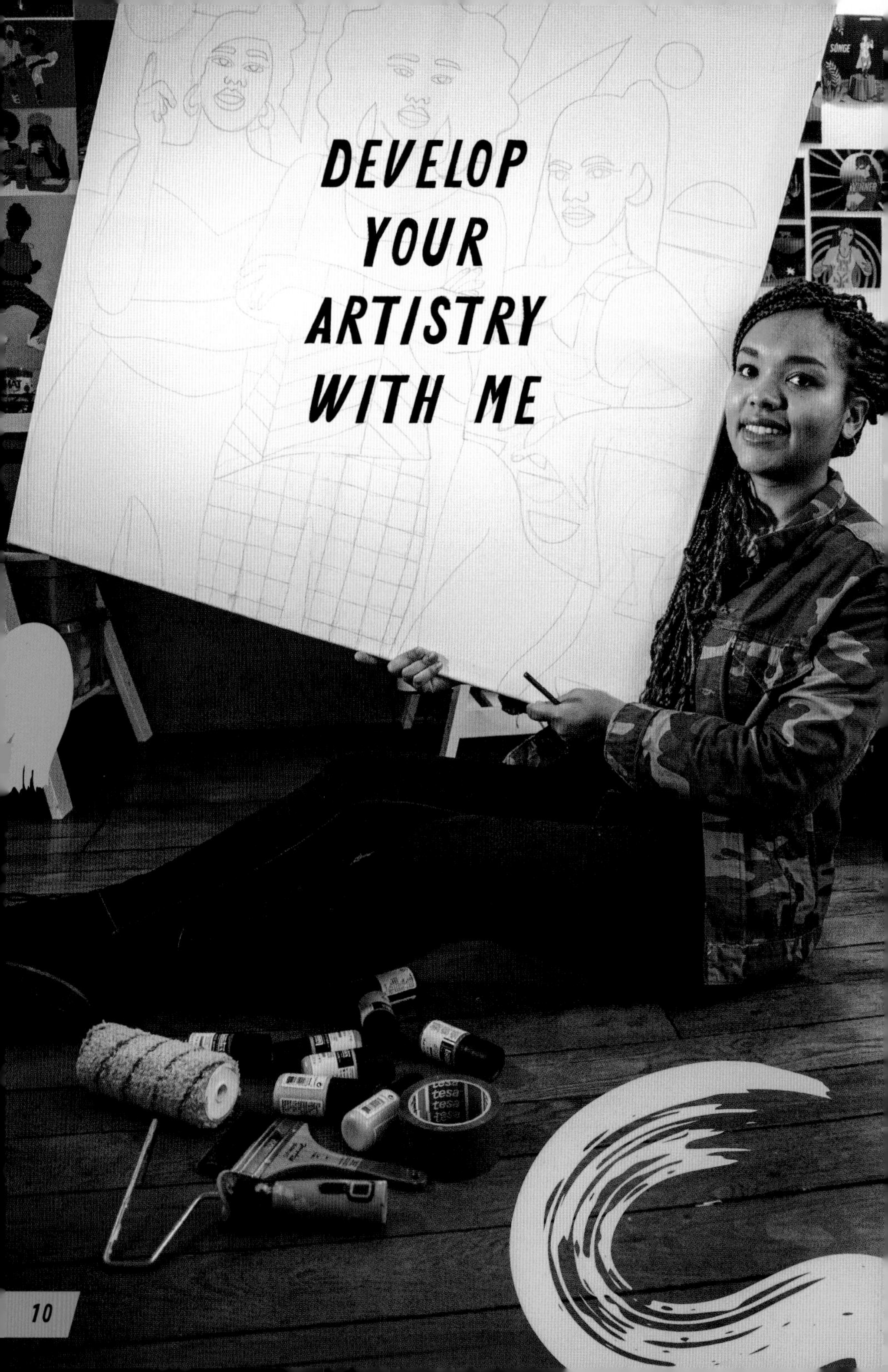

DO YOU HAVE IDEAS BUT NEED HELP FIGURING OUT WHERE TO START?

AS AN ARTIST, I have doubted myself over and over again. But with time and practice, I have become braver with my art. That's why I have written this book: to help you nurture your own creativity and find your own unique style. I'll be your guide on this artistic journey, sharing my own experiences and tips to help you develop your artistic style.

MAKING YOUR FIRST ARTISTIC CHOICES CAN BE TOUGH. Deciding on the graphic style, colors, shapes, and concepts for your project can feel overwhelming in the beginning. And it becomes even scarier when you share your work for the first time. You might worry how people will react to your project. But don't worry, and don't let this stop you! I experienced all of this when I started out, too. That's why I want to teach you how to develop resilience, which will allow you to ride the ups and downs of being a creative, and bounce back from any challenges you face. I'll help you discover your strengths and weaknesses so you can understand yourself better and remain strong when doubts try to get in your way.

Your art is a reflection of who you are and how you feel inside. When you feel confident and in tune with your inner self, it will be easier to unleash your creativity and make amazing art.

First of all, I want you to close your eyes and imagine you are feeling peaceful and content. Take a moment to picture it. Where are you? Now think about what you like and what makes you feel happy. What kind of art do you enjoy creating the most?

IN THIS BOOK, I WANT TO EMPOWER YOU AND SHOW YOU THAT ART CAN BE A WAY TO EXPRESS STRONG MESSAGES THAT CAN POSITIVELY IMPACT THE WORLD. LET'S GO!

HOW DID I GET STARTED?

LIFE IS ABOUT **MAKING DECISIONS**. **DON'T REGRET** MAKING CHOICES, AS YOU **NEVER KNOW** WHERE THEY WILL **LEAD** YOU.

YOU NEED A GROUP of people around you to uplift you and encourage you when making life decisions. Surrounding yourself with positive people who don't judge you, also known as your entourage, is important. Your entourage influences the choices you make for your future.

The first entourage who influenced me was my family. I didn't grow up in a creative family, but my parents encouraged me to go to art school. My mom and dad knew that becoming an **ARTIST WOULD BE CHALLENGING**, but they saw something in me. They always said that I was stubborn, persistent, and creative. Growing up, I'd spend all day in my room drawing and creating, so it was natural for me to decide to pursue a creative career.

When I was **17 YEARS OLD**, I was ready to approach the world with a new lens. I prepared a portfolio of drawings and pictures to apply for art schools. I knew from a young age that I wanted to study art, but not everyone knows so quickly. Maybe because they don't have a supportive entourage, or because they just aren't aware of their skills yet. It can take time to make such a big decision. I have some friends who studied at business school before they realized that they wanted to study art. It's never too late to change your mind!

Creative tip!

Who is in your entourage? Or who do you want to be in your entourage?

Think about people who make you feel good, support you, or inspire you. Perhaps they have skills you admire and want to learn from.

Consider finding a mentor; someone who is experienced, trustworthy, and willing to guide you. A mentor can be a teacher, an artist you admire, or someone older who has more life experience.

15

WE ARE ALL CREATIVE BEINGS.

WHATEVER YOU WANT TO BECOME IS POSSIBLE WITH A POSITIVE MINDSET AND THE RIGHT TOOLS.

AFTER SIX YEARS STUDYING, I got my masters degree in furniture and product design. But I wasn't ready to face the real world. I had too many questions in my head, such as: "How do I sell myself?", "How can I seem confident?", "How do I express my opinion?", "What kind of job do I want?" And then, "Am I even the right person for that job?. I felt more lost than ever.

FINDING MY WAY

When I was applying for junior furniture designer roles, the job advertisements all wanted *EXPERIENCED PEOPLE*. At 23 years old, I felt like I wasn't yet considered a grown-up. Being a young, Black female artist was rare where I came from, and I thought my opinion didn't carry much weight. When I was studying, I never saw any artists like me in books or museums. It was hard to believe I could make a living from being an artist. All the schools I went to were not enough to help me build a strong visual identity. The only solution was to teach myself more skills by experimenting and failing. It was scary, but I knew deep down that I would regret it if I didn't push through these uncertain times.

GRANTS

FINANCIAL SUPPORT

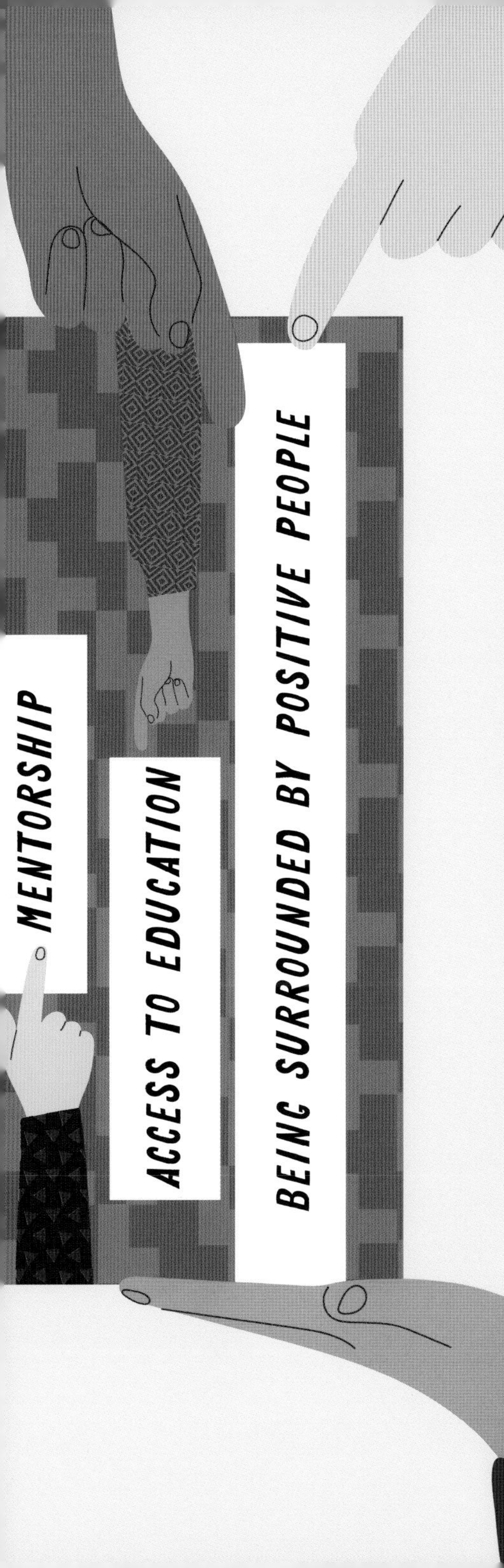

MENTORSHIP

ACCESS TO EDUCATION

BEING SURROUNDED BY POSITIVE PEOPLE

While in art school, I had developed various creative skills such as learning to brainstorm, creating photography, making concept designs, drawing, painting, and more. I thought, "What can I do with all of this knowledge?"

For inspiration, I read and watched stories about successful business people who used their special skills to create something of their own. I was fascinated by the idea of being self-made (which means to become successful through your own efforts). But these success stories frequently forget to mention that those who succeed often have certain advantages. They might have grown up in an environment that gave them opportunities to succeed, like money, access to education, stability, and more. It's not always just about working hard, or being more determined, or becoming smarter. Remember that there are structural and systematic inequalities at play that keep the same people in the same high positions from generation to generation.

CROWING UP

Different aspects of our identity can have an impact on our journey. My country and family gave me enough stability to take risks. In France, where I was born, education is free, including the art schools that I went to. The main challenge was passing the exam to get into art school. I studied in Dijon and Orléans; smaller cities where the cost of living was cheaper than Paris. My family is not wealthy. My mum was born in Ivory Coast and didn't have the opportunity to go to school. My dad grew up in France in a modest family. He excelled in school and became an engineer, working in that field for 30 years. My parents supported me financially while I was figuring out how to make a living as an artist. People don't often tell you when they receive help from family, because it breaks the idea that they became successful on their own. We must be honest about the advantages we have if we want to encourage more young people into the arts.

My cultural, societal, and family background led me to where I am today. I was able to take the risks I wanted to until they paid off. I wasn't predestined to be an artist, but I made choices and worked for it with the resources I had. Many people have had the same chances as me, but did they take the same path as me? No, because there is one more thing that you need: passion. The love I had for art as a kid kept growing and growing. All my experiences, like traveling and meeting different people, helped shape me into a better artist.

THE PEOPLE WHO SEEM LIKE *OVERNIGHT SUCCESSES* RARELY ARE. DIC DEEPER AND YOU'LL SEE THEY HAVE EITHER BEEN **WORKING HARD** FOR A VERY LONC TIME, OR HAVE HAD **SUPPORT** FROM FAMILY, OR SCHOLARSHIPS AND CRANTS.

TRAVEL CHANGED MY LIFE

When I was 22, I decided to go to a foreign country as an exchange student. I wanted to learn English and find new inspiration. My school in France had a partnership with the Fine Art and Design School of Copenhagen in Denmark, and I'd always loved Scandinavian design. I applied to the exchange programme and was invited to join it from January 2013 to July 2013. It happened so fast, and I was excited to explore a country I had never visited before. While in Copenhagen, I met lots of students from other countries. It was amazing! I made friends who were studying different things, from architecture and music, to theater, fine arts, and design. We would talk about our creativity and how we developed it in our own countries. It was so interesting to hear their stories! I started to open up to new people and learn English; I was really eager to gain knowledge and discover the world. It was a truly special experience that made me feel alive and inspired in every way possible.

This new experience definitely changed my artistic journey. At the end of my exchange, I fell in love with a Danish man who was studying music at a school near mine. I had to go back to France to finish the last year of my masters, but I promised him that I would go back and live with him. In August 2014, I moved back to Copenhagen and stayed until 2021.

When I moved back to Copenhagen, things were different for me. I had finished school and was now a graduate. I was ready to find a job and become part of Danish society. I spent six months sending out my CV and my portfolio to furniture design studios, but it was tough. No one wanted to hire me, and I couldn't figure out why.

Looking back, I realized that my portfolio had more illustrations than actual design concepts. I had been fooling myself thinking that studying furniture design would make it easier to find a job than being a painter or illustrator. I needed new projects for my portfolio, but the only way to get them was to do an internship at a design studio. The problem was that internships in Denmark didn't pay, so I would be working for free.

I LIVED IN COPENHAGEN FOR EIGHT YEARS

I LOVED CYCLING IN THE CHARMING STREETS

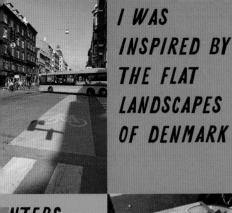

I WAS
INSPIRED BY
THE FLAT
LANDSCAPES
OF DENMARK

NTERS
ERE COLD,
MMERS
ERE
RIGHT

Exercise

How to develop ideas

- First, write down your ideas so you can easily come back to them.

- Brainstorm your ideas. Write down any words that come to your mind. Dedicate time to doing research. This can be online, in books, and outside in places such as museums, exhibitions, events, cinemas, or with people.

- Write down everything you learned during your research. This will help you to develop your idea and confront it with other ideas you have.

- Choose a few people to talk to about your project. This will help you learn how to communicate your ideas and bring in more viewpoints and feedback that can enrich your thoughts.

- Try to consistently sketch and make images while you explore your project.

- Keep the vibes positive while you're in the process of creating.

- Breathe and take breaks. You need the energy to produce original ideas.

If you follow these steps, you'll be on the right path to achieving your goals!

I stayed in Copenhagen for eight years and during that time, I learned a lot about myself as an entrepreneur and an artist.

An old classmate who was also living in Copenhagen and I co-funded a design studio. We created eco-friendly products and stationery, such as wrapping paper and sketchbooks. We had both struggled to find a paid job, and we liked the idea of working together.

We sold our products to shops and at Christmas markets. Working together posed some challenges, because we had similar skills, and it was difficult to decide who would take on which tasks. There was the creative, the business, and communication sides to look after, but we never could figure out who would do which tasks. The most successful teams usually have members with different and complementary roles. After two years, we were not making any money, and my business partner decided to move back to France to find a job.

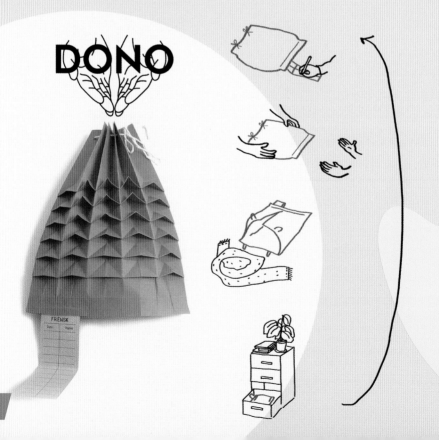

My next project was to create a design solution for bike parking during events in Danish cities. This opportunity came about when I met my future business partner at a competition called a "Hackathon" in the summer of 2014. Hackathons are events where people come together to develop new solutions to problems collaboratively. My partner had business skills and I had a design background, so we complemented each other. Our idea involved creating a rental service for a nested system of bicycle parking (see picture) that event organizers and local councils across Denmark would pay to hire. My role was to create the visual communications to show how the product worked, from 3D renderings to presentations for pitching to investors.

We won the competition and then were given the opportunity to show our solution at COP21 (COP stands for Conference of the Parties, referring to the countries that have signed up to the 1992 United Nations Framework Convention on Climate Change) in Paris. After we showed our solution, we had a lot of positive feedback, so we decided to continue working on it. We got noticed by the Roskilde Festival (the biggest music festival in Denmark), and soon, we were working with several different festivals and events.

Our product was getting popular, but things were tough, because the event organizers and local councils didn't want to pay, and the costs of transport, workforce, and our limited skills were preventing us from continuing the adventure. We weren't making any money from it. This difficult time created distance between me and my business partner. Our interests changed, and our relationship got worse. In the end, we decided to go our separate ways.

DOUBLE U, A BICYCLE PARKING SOLUTION FOR EVENTS IN DENMARK

DOUBLE U
BIKE PARKING

LEARNING LESSONS

These early entrepreneurial experiences were necessary for me to become the independent artist I am today. Through this entrepreneurial journey, I discovered who I was. I saw my capabilities and my limits. I became confident about presenting an idea to people I didn't know. And I learned a lot about communicating and negotiating. Starting an entrepreneurial journey is an act of bravery; I had to accept that anything can happen. I made mistakes but kept persisting. Overall, I learned that failing projects shouldn't feel like a personal failure but more like an opportunity to learn.

Step by step, I found my own path and gained confidence. I didn't dream of being an ambitious entrepreneur. For me, it was about surviving and not giving up on my artistic passion. I didn't have any other choice but to keep going and see where my creative skills would take me. Even though I didn't have a clear plan, I wasn't stressed about my uncertain situation. This mindset allowed me to explore and discover what I was capable of.

Throughout my journey, I had mentors from different industries who taught me about creative entrepreneurship. Unfortunately, all my businesses failed. I invested my time, money, and strained my friendships. But despite the setbacks, I developed resilience and determination. It's important to remember that many successful creative entrepreneurs have faced failures before finding that one business idea that takes off.

Exercise

What projects would you like to start with?

If you're thinking about starting a creative project, it's great to have people join you. It makes the journey more enjoyable, and you'll learn a lot about yourself along the way. You can discover your leadership skills, learn how to work well in a team, and understand how to organize tasks and create schedules. Working with partners will help you identify your strengths and weaknesses, and together, you'll learn things you never even imagined. So, reach out to someone who might be interested and embark on this creative entrepreneurial adventure together!

AN IDENTITY CRISIS

After the series of unfortunate entrepreneurial events I shared with you earlier, I started to feel homesick. I missed my friends and my family back in France. Winters in Denmark were long and dark, and I felt lonely. Being away from home for so long made it challenging to understand what my identity was as an artist. I couldn't figure out what my artistic purpose was and every time I tried, I kept on failing.

I began to wonder, "Who am I now?", "How do people see me?", "Am I still French-Ivorian?", and "What part of me am I losing by trying to assimilate to Danish society?" Denmark, with its population of around 6 million people, felt like a small country to me. While the Danish people were generally welcoming, finding true acceptance was difficult.

When I moved to Denmark, I knew that I'd be seen as different because of the color of my skin, but I felt it would be an advantage to be different. However, after living in Denmark for a year, I started to feel the impact of being culturally dissimilar and sounding distinct because of my accent. It became challenging for me to feel included in Danish society. I tried to integrate by learning to speak Danish and about the culture.

AM I STILL FRENCH-IVORIAN?

WHO AM I NOW?

But I felt demoralized when Danish people only chose to respond to me in English instead of engaging in conversation in Danish.

Denmark is famous for its *"hygge"* lifestyle, which means a cosy and comfortable way of living. However, I've noticed that this idea can sometimes exclude others. Hygge is all about familiarity and comfort, and I found that being around someone different can make some Danish people feel uneasy. This made it challenging for me to make friends in Denmark. Most of my friends in Denmark actually came from countries other than Denmark. I still feel disappointed that I wasn't able to make more friends from Denmark. I truly believe that having new friends from different countries and cultures can help solve many problems in our societies.

FINDING MYSELF

I sensed that if I wanted to truly settle in Copenhagen, I would have to make compromises and let go of a part of myself. Otherwise, I would always feel on the outside. However, I wasn't ready for that yet, as I was still in the process of discovering my identity as a Black, French woman. There was a lingering sense of shame, because my mother never shared her past and her Ivorian culture with me. It made me feel like I was missing a part of who I truly was.

When I first started studying at art school, I centered my art around my biracial identity, and I wanted to discover more about my African heritage through my art. Questioning my identity happened early on for me.

I have a vivid memory of being seven years old and the other children at school putting insects in my afro hair because they found it ugly. Both children and teachers mocked me. Because I felt so different, I asked my mom to relax my hair to try and stop my classmates from mocking me. I was ashamed.

As a teenager, things became even more complex for me. I had dreams of being white so that people wouldn't label me as hideous. I didn't quite fit in with either Black or white kids because of my mixed heritage. I never felt comfortable in my own skin until I turned 18 and enrolled in art school. There, I met people who looked different, and I realized that no one was judging them based on their appearance. It was in that environment that I finally began to embrace who I truly was.

Being a creative person is, for me, a way to communicate about subjects I would never see represented visually. I had always dreamed of seeing Black girls being strong, taking the lead, and embracing their identity with pride. Throughout my upbringing, I looked up to African-American icons like Destiny's Child, The Jackson 5, Tia and Tamera Mowry, Beyoncé, Aaliyah, Ciara, and many others who became my heroes and role models. They inspired me to believe in myself and celebrate my own uniqueness.

HOMECOMING AND FINDING A STYLE

One day in October 2017, when I was 27 years old and still living in Copenhagen, I stumbled upon some old drawings from my school days. As I looked at them again, I realized that I'd never had the opportunity to explore the questions I had about my identity through those drawings. This time, though, I felt determined to find answers.

I noticed many artists and illustrators sharing their work on Instagram, and it inspired me. I felt that there was a lack of art featuring and representing people of color, and I wanted to change that. So, I picked up my graphic tablet and started drawing whatever came to mind. I created Black characters with strong expressions and vibrant, catchy slogans. My art became a way for me to address the lack of visibility and representation for Black and brown people. It was my voice filling the empty spaces and loudly expressing what I'd felt for so long but couldn't say out loud due to fear and shame. Through my art, I found a sense of purpose and the courage to embrace who I truly was.

NOVEMBER 2017

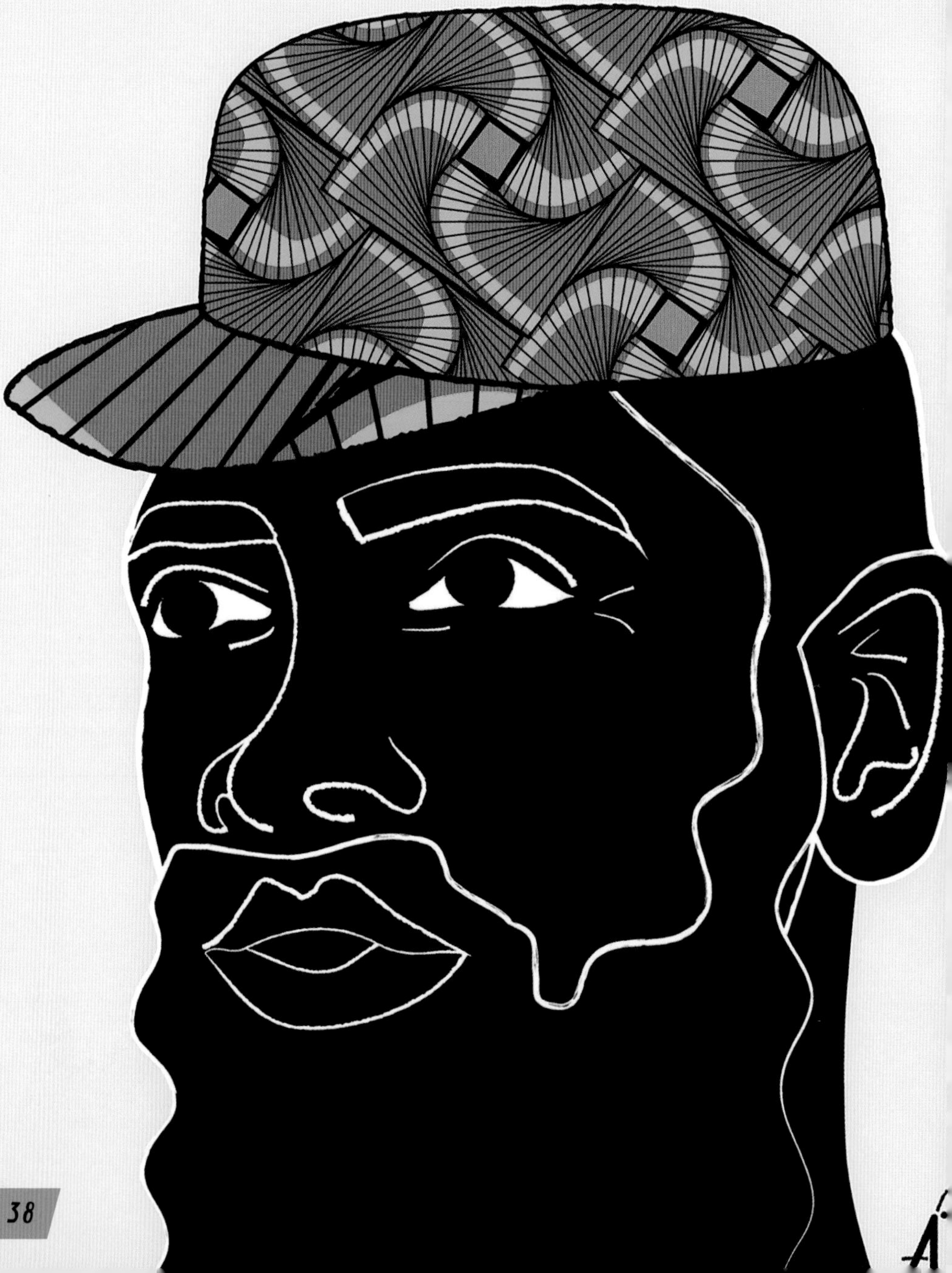

JANUARY 2018

BLACK
IS
VIBRANT

MAKING CONNECTIONS ONLINE

After I shared my first Instagram post, it didn't take long for people to discover my work, share it, and connect with me. Within just six months, a community of 10,000 people from all over the world followed me on Instagram. I had spoken my truth, and it resonated deeply with others. Many people saw themselves in my stories. Like me, they too had grown up feeling ashamed and with complicated feelings about their heritage.

I kept sharing my art on Instagram. At first, I used plain gray backgrounds, not the bright colors I use now. Then, in 2018, I had my first exhibition in Copenhagen. That's when I started using more vibrant colors and my message became clearer. I sought to create a joyful protest against racism through my art. Using bright colors, I wanted to catch people's attention and tell stories about Black people who are often overlooked.

The followers on my Instagram page grew month after month, and soon I started to receive commissions (requests from companies for me to make art specifically for them) via DMs. People were offering me paid work! At first, it was small businesses, and then it escalated to bigger companies like Apple and Facebook.

NEW MESSAGE

COPENHAGEN 2018

COPENHAGEN 2016

SAYING GOODBYE

In 2021, after eight years, I left Denmark and returned to France. My time in Denmark helped me become braver and prouder of my French and biracial identity. It was there that I truly discovered myself. During my journey in Denmark, I faced challenges and difficult times, but I learned to be resilient and strong. I had to say goodbye to some friendships and relationships, but it was the best time of my life, and I am grateful for every moment I spent there.

COPENHAGEN 2020

LIFE IS A JOURNEY, AND THE JOURNEY IS ONGOING!

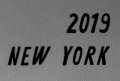

IN SHORT

Creativity has become an essential part of my life and something I can't live without. When I was younger, I used to think that I couldn't take the lead or be bold. But through my travels, discoveries, and even my failures, I gained more confidence and found the strength to overcome my fears. These experiences have unlocked the power of creativity within me, shaping who I am today.

Don't worry if it goes wrong. That's totally normal. Just keep on going.

As you gain creative experiences, you will start to grow. Along the way, meet friends, initiate projects, and travel to unlock your creativity. Remember, if you don't actively practice and work on your craft, nothing will come to you magically.

And most importantly, enjoy the process!

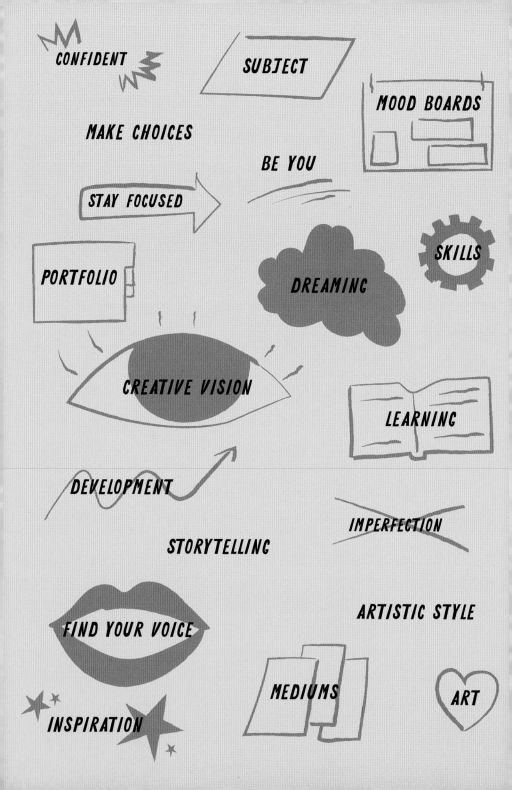

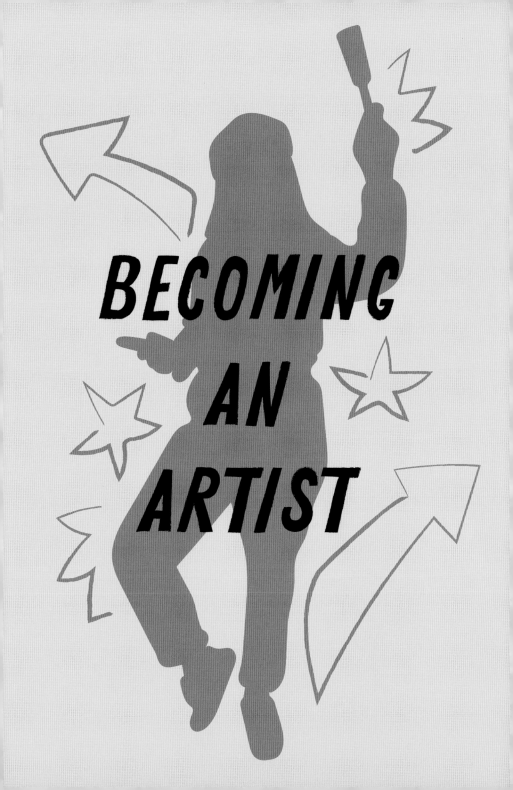

LIFE IS ABOUT MAKING CHOICES. YOU NEVER KNOW WHERE THEY MIGHT LEAD YOU.

GIVE A VOICE TO YOUR ART

ART COMES FROM YOU

Who are you? What do you love to do? What drives you? These are tough questions, because we're always discovering new things about ourselves. You can choose who you want to become by following paths you enjoy. Your passion will fuel you, giving you excitement and making you unstoppable.

When you love what you do, something magical happens. You let go of worries and focus on your passion. Your art will reflect who you are, your story, hopes, and sensitivities. Over time, your projects will help you discover yourself.

Sometimes you won't know the reasons for your choices right away. It's like solving a jigsaw without knowing the final image. Embrace finding your artistic voice. Stay optimistic, don't limit your creativity, and express your emotions – revolt, ecstasy, heartbreak, anger, hope, and whatever else you feel.

Creative tip!

Discovering your passion

If you want to be an artist because you love creating art and telling visual stories, then you should ask yourself the following questions:

- Why am I interested in creating art?
- What was my first experience with art?
- Which artists am I influenced by?
- What will be the subject of my art? And why?

When you have a better understanding of who you are and what you like, you will know what you want to pursue with your art.

STAY TRUE TO YOURSELF

YOU MAY ADMIRE CERTAIN ARTISTS AND WISH YOU HAD THEIR STYLE, BUT DON'T TRY TO COPY THEM TO MAKE A LIVING. YOU'RE CAPABLE OF CREATING YOUR OWN UNIQUE STYLE. THE INTERNET IS A SMALL WORLD, AND PEOPLE CAN TELL IF YOU'RE IMITATING SOMEONE ELSE. I'VE SEEN THIS HAPPEN TO OTHER ARTISTS. INSTEAD OF COPYING, EMBRACE WHO YOU ARE, AND DEVELOP YOUR OWN STYLE. THAT WILL BRING YOU MUCH MORE PRIDE THAN COPYING SOMEONE ELSE'S WORK.

When I first started illustration, I was inspired by the artists I loved and tried to emulate their styles. By practicing and exploring different styles, I was trying to uncover my own.

However, I never published this work online or ever pretended it was my own work. And at some point, I was limited by copying others, and I realized new ideas needed to come from me. I couldn't progress and communicate a powerful message through other people's artwork. So, for three years, I kept trying different styles. I used watercolor and colored pencils before I started experimenting with digital art.

Just like a chef with a recipe, I listed ingredients (colors, shapes, lettering) and combined them together to make a new dish (style). My new dish began to improve day after day.

I found my own artistic style and gained confidence when I overcame my fear of what other people would think. I was ready to talk about and fight for my artistic vision. I spoke my own truth, as my art came from my heart, and reflected my identity, my battles, my travels, my family, my education, my pain, my preferences, and my hopes. My artistic voice became a strong identity shaped by these aspects. I aimed to reveal my humanity and vulnerability through my work, connecting with others who could relate.

I wanted my art to be eye-catching. I used contrast to communicate important messages about anti-racism, feminism, and multiculturalism. These issues matter to me, and I wanted to raise awareness and spark conversations through my work. And that is how I started to develop my artistic voice. I was inspired by many things which I combined in my work, including films by the director Spike Lee, art movements and styles like Constructivism and Bauhaus, artists from Picasso, Le Corbusier, and Monet, to Basquiat, Andy Warhol, and Obey, as well as contemporary artists and designers, such as Kehinde Wiley, Kerry James Marshall, Matali Crasset, Patricia Urquiola, Lisa Congdon, Andrea Pippins, Malika Favre, Olimpia Zagnoli, Sara Andreasson, Egle Zvirblyte, Petra Eriksson, Karabo Poppy, Timothy Goodman, Inès Longevial, and Nina Chanel Abney.

Exercise

How to explore creatively

Grab a notebook and pen. Every day for a week, write down words and draw things you like. Analyze your week of doodling and see what stands out the most. Make a list of artists who inspire you, and think about why you like them. Is it the use of colors, shapes, structures, or lines in their art?

What are your hobbies besides art?

Embrace your uniqueness. People will appreciate seeing your authentic self through your art. Talk about your ideas and share what you've been creating lately. Show your passion and discuss your artistic vision with others. This will help you become more confident in defending your ideas and shaping your artistic vision.

DEVELOP A CREATIVE VISION

A unique visual style is created by the combination of subject, style, medium, and the artist's skills.

THE SUBJECT. Art is a narration, as it tells stories. Most of the time, it is the story of the artist. We are drawn to create visuals based on our lives, what we have experienced, and what has influenced us.

THE STYLE. Your artistic style is the unique way you express yourself through your work. It can be abstract, realistic, or geometric, and it reflects your artistic voice. Consider the shapes, dimensions, perspectives, color palette, texture, patterns, composition, and movement in your visuals to define your distinctive style. Explore and experiment with these elements to create a visual language that truly represents you.

THE MEDIUM. These are the tools you use to give expression and form to your artistic voice. It can be the brushes you use on your iPad, the paint you use, or it can be the support you use to paint a mural or a canvas. The medium influences the style and tone of the artwork, contributing to its unique character.

YOUR SKILLS. Your unique skills and talents help you to develop your style and create a rich and complex body of work. While you don't have to be the best drawer or photographer, having a good understanding of the fundamentals and finding ways to express your creative ideas is important. Keep experimenting with your skills. For example, being good at drawing realistically is great, but you might need to express an idea through drawing. So sometimes your art might become more abstract.

Finding your individual artistic path can be daunting. You may feel like everything has been done before, and there's no room for you. But that's not true! We all have a particular story worth listening to. As we grow, our vision of the world unfolds, and so does the art we make. Before discovering my style, I explored different colors, shapes, and subjects. As an artist, my approach keeps evolving and taking new forms, and it's always open to transformation. I find joy in this continuous search for creativity, and I hope you will too.

TELL A STORY

To create a meaningful impact with your art, it's important to tell your story in a compelling way that captures people's attention. Use techniques like paintings, photographs, videos, words, graphics, and drawings that you enjoy. Artists have the power to illuminate the world through their artwork, which is often complex, bold, and textured, adding depth and substance to their stories. Defining your purpose as an artist influences the creative process and helps your artwork stand out while also building a community around it.

Creative tip!

Think about your artistic intentions

What do you hope to communicate to people through your artwork that they may not have seen before? Or what do you like to see for yourself?

Are there any specific skills you are interested in learning to enhance your style and make it even more special?

CREATE A MOOD BOARD OF INSPIRATIONAL IMAGERY

A mood board is a special board of ideas that inspires you and can help you plan your art project. Gather pictures, colors, and words to give you ideas and guide your creative process. When making a mood board, I look at the artists I like from different disciplines, such as architecture for the textures, and textile design for the clothes, and so on. I often use Pinterest to brainstorm ideas.

Exercise

How to make your own mood board:

1. Brainstorm your theme with some keywords related to the ideas you have in mind. Online image search engines, such as Google, Getty, Unsplash, Pinterest, or Instagram can help you gather some visuals. If you're not drawn to a particular idea yet, look through magazines or books related to your art field and see what catches your attention.

2. Gather your inspirations from the previous step and think creatively to find more. Look at movie scenes, fashion shoots, old illustrations, artworks, fabrics, colors, architecture, objects, and clothes. Don't forget about typography, too! Different fonts can convey different feelings, so use them to showcase keywords or quotes that relate to your theme.

3. Review and organize your board. You might have collected a lot of things, so choose the images and samples that go well together and show your unique style. Make sure the colors on your board look good together. If you're making a digital board, use a color picker tool to select five important colors from the images to make swatches. If you're making a physical board, pick up some paint or fabric swatches to match the colors.

CHALLENGE YOURSELF TO EXPLORE NEW DISCIPLINES

YOU DON'T NEED TO BE GOOD AT EVERYTHING

It's okay if you don't master every artistic skill. Instead of becoming a master of each one, I learned to adapt different mediums, like photography, drawing, and animation, to express my creative ideas. I know how to use a camera so that I can take pictures of my work, my studio and myself, and I know how to use the Adobe Creative Suite to create digital artworks. I'm no expert, but I can make things the way I want.

I love to experiment with my art, and over time, I've learned different skills, like film editing, painting, photography, digital illustration, animation, branding, and even speaking in front of a camera or an audience. In art school, I was encouraged to explore many techniques rather than focusing on just one. I was educated as a multidisciplinary artist, which is why I'm not afraid to try new things and continue building my skills.

MY FIRST TIMES:

PAINTING A MURAL

Once, I had the opportunity to paint on a 158 ft-long wall in Paris. It was my first time doing something like that, and it made me feel a little uncomfortable. Thankfully, Art Azoï—the association who hired me for the project—provided me with four people and all the materials I needed to make it a success. It was reassuring to have their support and expertise.

GIVING A WORKSHOP IN FRONT OF AN AUDIENCE

All my life, I believed I was a shy person, but my artistic work helped me realize that I'm actually the opposite. It gave me the confidence, strength, and ability to speak and share my work with others, which is incredibly rewarding and thrilling for me.

CREATING AN ANIMATION

I never learned animation at school, but one day, I decided to make an animation for a friend's music video and learn more about the software Adobe After Effects. It was tough, and I wanted to give up, but I persevered, watched YouTube tutorials, and completed it with pride. Still today, I continue to improve my technique and embrace my mistakes, which adds a uniqueness to my work.

CREATE A PORTFOLIO

A portfolio is a collection of your best work that showcases your skills, talents, and creativity. It typically includes a variety of visual materials such as artwork, designs, photographs, or samples of your creative projects. Having a portfolio will help potential clients to understand what you are capable of creating.

I want to emphasize that having different skills helps to develop a range of artworks and get more commissions. Clients may have larger projects in mind and may want you to go beyond just one skill. That's why it's good to experiment with different techniques, even if you're not an expert. Don't hesitate to display your abilities proudly and show what you can do. Clients might assume that if they don't see something in your portfolio, you can't do it, and that's a missed opportunity.

Creative tip!

Imagine your dream work project

Before you create your portfolio, think about which projects you would like people or clients to ask you about. Do you like to represent people? Nature? Geometric shapes? Letters? Do you like painting, or do you like digital work? By creating various works, people will be able to see your skills. Try to think ahead and decide if you may get tired of drawing only one thing so that you can show other skills in your portfolio.

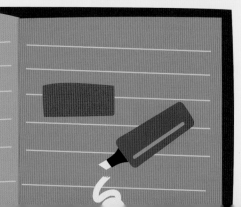

COVER

- Your name and your skills

- Your website and social media

- A picture. This could be of you in the studio creating, one of your favorite projects, or a collection of your works

CONTENTS

- About yourself

- Projects sorted by category e.g. illustrations of people, landscapes, animals and abstract, lettering, animations, murals etc.

- Your contact details

ABOUT ME

- Who are you?
  What's your art about?
  What's your speciality?

- Education

- Experiences

- Major projects

- Exhibitions

- Workshops

- Press

PROJECT 01

Illustration

- Subject: What is it about? Why did you make it? What is the impact?

- Technique: How did you make it?

- Year (include this if you want to show the evolution of your work)

PROJECT 02

Animation

- Show your process, inspiration, sketches, search for colors, and motion effects

- Explain your ideas: what, why, how

- Give a link to a video, if possible

CONTACT

- Name

- Email address

- Website

- Social media

STAY FOCUSED

In today's world, we are surrounded by an enormous amount of information, and social media can often distract us from finding inspiration.

When I look online and see so many impressive artworks, I often feel overwhelmed and uninspired. It feels like everything has been done already, and I question how I can make my work stand out. I begin to doubt myself and my work and find it difficult to focus.

One thing I know is that I must stop using my phone and computer so much. It's important for me to go out and to take breaks, to visit museums and theaters, to see live music, and meet up with friends. And when I'm still stuck for inspiration, I lay on my couch, close my eyes, listen to music, and reflect on what I have experienced recently. Ideas begin to form in my head, and I'm able to start envisioning them.

Exercise

How to conquer the chaos

This is a technique I use when I feel overwhelmed. Grab a sheet of paper and a pen. Make sure to put your phone and computer away. Close your eyes and start to draw what comes to mind. While drawing, you might slowly go into a zone where your creative choices become more intuitive. Usually when I do this, my mind becomes peaceful, and I feel absorbed in what I am drawing. Time is suspended. I'm in the present and in a joyous state of mind.

WHEN EVERYTHING GOES DIFFERENTLY THAN PLANNED

Even when unexpected events change your plans, it's important not to panic. When starting on your independent creative journey, things often don't go as planned initially, and it's natural to feel like your efforts aren't yielding immediate results. However, remember that success takes time and dedication. Stay persistent, keep pushing forwards, and maintain a positive mindset. The fruits of your hard work will eventually show themselves, so trust in the process and give it your all.

Creative tip!

Learning from experience

Think of a creative idea you've had recently. Did everything go the way you hoped for? If yes, can you say why? If not, what went wrong? How do you cope with a plan not going the way you wanted? Did you talk about it with anyone? You could reach out to your mentor and explain your situation. They may be able to give you some good advice and support.

IN SHORT

Developing a creative voice is like unlocking a superpower. The creative process may feel daunting, but once you embrace and harness your unique superpower, you will feel strong and unstoppable.

Your artistic voice is your story, so don't be ashamed of it. The fear of sharing stops many of us from expressing our creativity. You don't need an impressive story to make art. We all have something worth sharing. Maybe not everyone will relate to your vision, but some will.

Remember, you can make art about anything! You don't have to follow the latest trends just because it is what works the best. Maybe you will invent a whole new creative world. There are so many topics to be inspired by, such as love, fashion, family, memories, daydreams, hopes, culture, food, and more. What matters the most is the energy and passion you put into your work.

Once you are comfortable with your artistic voice, you can focus on how to make this voice a business.

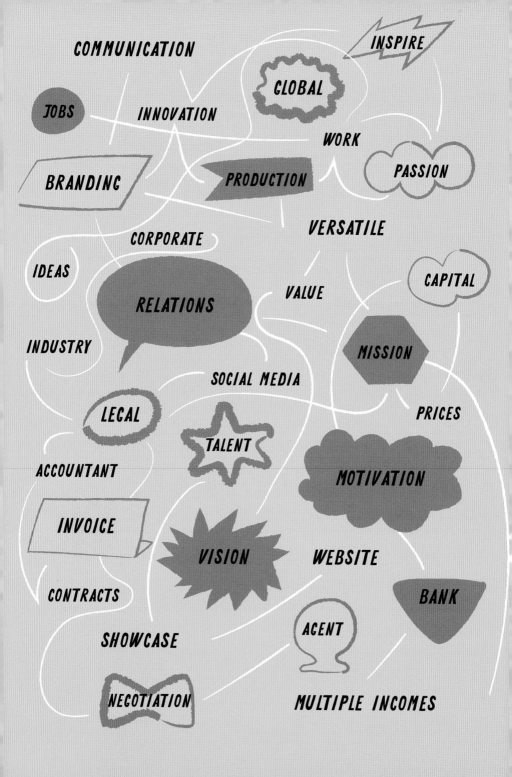

A CREATIVE BUSINESS

IT'S A JOB TO BE CREATIVE

People often romanticize creative professions, particularly those that involve working independently. Whether you're an illustrator or a writer, being your own boss means taking full responsibility for your business and its success.

The truth is, making art as a hobby is different from making it your job. As a professional, you have to handle more than just being creative, and you have many roles to play: artist, photographer, social media manager, brand strategist, agent, secretary, accountant, manager, and artistic director. You need to take care of responsibilities like making money to support your career and life. It's necessary and can't be avoided.

I juggle all these roles to keep my creative business running smoothly.

I have to negotiate fees for projects, maintain my website, publish on social media networks, respond to emails and calls from clients, read work contracts, take care of my finances, organize events, and more. And lastly, I need to set aside creative days for my own personal artwork. It's essential!

One of the most important but hardest things is to develop a sustainable business. Art is an industry like any other industry; it involves dealing with money and marketing. But the good news is that all the admin and organizing becomes easier with practice. Creative professions are demanding and stressful, but they are also fabulous, because you get to do something you really love!

HOW TO BRAND YOUR ART

How do you present yourself as an artist to a crowd? What do you want to be known for with your art? Your story is just as important as the art you create. And by branding yourself right, you will likely increase the work you get.

People are interested in getting to know you, so don't hesitate to share your story. Your personal journey and experiences provide valuable insights into your art. Remember, you don't need to be good at everything. It's enough to have a great story to tell and use your creative skills to be compelling.

Communication plays a crucial role in your journey as a creative entrepreneur. It allows you to express your artistic identity. You can use type, color, pattern, illustration, and texture to convey a thoughtful and purposeful message. This will help you attract the right clients, inspire them to work with you, and get you to where you want to be, faster.

YOU ARE THE BRAND

Your personal brand should be a strong representation of who you are and what you do. It's a mix of your art, passion, and goals, and it's important to let others know about your accomplishments and talents so you can find new opportunities.

SHOWING WHO YOU ARE WILL LEAD YOU TO CREATE GENUINE CONNECTIONS WITH POTENTIAL CLIENTS.

Your brand will connect with the people who truly appreciate and understand your art, but not everyone will be your ideal audience, and that's okay. It's important to be genuine and authentic. Don't be afraid to share your journey, including both the successes and challenges, as it shows your true character and honesty.

PERSONAL PROJECTS TO DEVELOP YOUR ART

As an artist, personal projects were crucial in developing my career. When I was feeling homesick in Denmark, I started creating art from my heart without any specific plans or clients. I found my artistic voice because of these personal projects, which eventually led to a professional career in art. By organizing my schedule and finances, I could also fund and pursue those personal projects that inspired me.

DEVELOPING YOUR ART IS ESSENTIAL TO SHOWCASE NEW SKILLS TO YOUR CLIENTS.

Being an artist requires practice, and personal projects are a great way to try out new things. They also help to reenergize me and often lead to new assignments or new ways of earning money, too.

While working on commissions, remember to nourish your personal projects and keep trying new ideas.

CREATE A FOLLOWING

Some people fear showing their work to an audience because they feel vulnerable. For others, it's an exciting step towards creating a community around their work.

You might have seen methods and tips to gain thousands of subscribers on YouTube or Instagram. But really, there is no quick fix, and it takes time and dedication. To grow your following online, it is important to understand why people would want to follow you and your work. Your community might have expectations about the type of content they would like to see. As well as being creative, it helps to learn marketing and communication skills to entertain your audience. Test your content by publishing images or videos to see what receives the most attention. Your followers might give you feedback that can help you find your work direction. There are many different kinds of followers. Some are non-active while others are active admirers who like, share, and comment on your posts. Some will be big fans (customers), or people from within the art industry who might want to commission your work.

GATHER PEOPLE AROUND YOUR WORK AND CREATE A MEANINGFUL COMMUNITY.

DO YOU HAVE TO POST REGULARLY?

Social media platforms like Instagram want users to publish content and scroll continuously. Sometimes, I see creators posting two to three times a day and picking up 100k followers in a year. However, quantity doesn't always mean quality, and I prefer to have a few engaged followers rather than lots of people who don't interact with my content. Posting regularly helps you connect with your audience, but it's important to provide valuable content to gain followers and engagement.

Growing on any social media platform doesn't happen magically. It requires hard work, originality, and finding a strategy that works for you. Social media is always changing, so you need to create content that hooks people and gets them interested in your unique style.

THE IMPACT OF SOCIAL MEDIA ON THE ILLUSTRATION INDUSTRY

I know that my work was noticed thanks to Instagram. Therefore, I believe in the good side of social media platforms. Once you find a style and you get noticed, you'll be able to find people who love your work and convert those likes into paid work. Perhaps, you might meet a new community of artists like yourself!

I also understand the downsides of social media. It can sometimes make us feel down, especially when we focus too much on likes and comments, or when we don't get the desired attention.

It's better to have quality engagement on your social media. You don't have to follow a trend just because it gets more likes. Instead, focus on yourself and your artistic vision. What do you like? What do you want to put out into the world? Stay true to yourself and focus on that.

MY EXPERIENCE WITH SOCIAL MEDIA

In late 2017, while living in Denmark, I was part of a Facebook group called "Women of Colour Copenhagen". We organized events where we shared our experiences and imagined creative projects. Thanks to these hangouts, I began to grow an online following. I published new illustrative narratives about Black hair, how society sees our hair, and how I feel about my own hair. My online posts reached a big audience who related to my stories, and thanks to the algorithm, they became even more far-reaching. Soon, people began sharing my work, and eventually, I was commissioned to do illustrations.

TALENT GOES BEYOND SOCIAL MEDIA

I was lucky, but the reality is that only a few people become professional artists and make a living from their art. Simply drawing is not enough; you need something unique and original to stand out. Developing your originality takes time and effort. Remember: getting your art noticed is hard work, and someone who might seem like an overnight success online often has years of effort behind them.

Exercise

How to captivate and connect on Instagram

Instagram is a great platform to connect with people and showcase your art. If you learn to use it well, you can put yourself out there and make a career from your passion.

Here are the steps to reach a new audience:

1. Figure out who your ideal audience is and what interests them. Share content that connects with them, whether it's fun, inspirational, or educational. What are your interests in life, and what are your themes?

2. Create a profile that shows who you are and what you do. Include a biography, links, stories, and your first posts.

3. Take daily action to grow your community and engagement. Share different types of content, like illustrations, behind-the-scenes photos, animations, visual stories, and mood boards.

4. Interact with your audience. This could mean:

- Sharing stories about the real you. You might include images from behind the scenes so that people can connect with you better.

- Streaming live videos so you can interact with your followers.

- Creating groups on topics you care about.

- Connecting with your community. You could contact other artists and ask to meet them in real life, or talk about what you do online to build new relationships.

WEBSITE

Your website is super important for your business. It's like an online home where people learn about you and your art. Make it simple to navigate and use meaningful pictures to connect with your audience. First, use a white or one-color background so that your artwork will stand out more. I suggest using only two fonts and making sure you have high-quality photos of you, your work, and your workspace. A good website will help you to attract more customers, as people will know how to contact you! It is an opportunity to showcase your brand to potential clients and make a great first impression. When people find you online, they will become interested in what you do and want to know more.

ON YOUR WEBSITE, YOU SHOULD PRESENT WHO YOU ARE, WHAT YOU DO, AND HOW TO CONTACT YOU.

MENU   WORK - CONTACT - ABOUT - SHOP

YOUR NAME
OR NICKNAME

WHAT YOU DO

SOCIAL MEDIA LINKS

RECENT WORK

HOW TO SET PRICES?

Setting prices as an illustrator means deciding how much to charge for your artwork or illustration services. It can be a daunting task, but there are some ways to make it easier. First, stand by your art and do not give it away for free. You are creating a business to make a living, so you need to be a good marketer while also learning how to sell your art and negotiate payment for your work.

Some clients may offer you "exposure", which means they will spread the word about your work and bring you new customers, but they won't offer financial payment. This might sound tempting, but consider how you'll pay your bills if you don't receive money for your art.

Figuring out a deal can be difficult when you're new to the industry. That's why having an agent can be helpful. But not everyone has an agent, so don't worry if you make mistakes at first. When I first started, I made lots of mistakes. Just keep in mind the value of the work you are creating and how the client will use it.

When it comes to asking for payment, it's important to be fair and value your work appropriately. Here are some things to consider:

NEGOTIATE IN WRITING RATHER THAN IN PERSON TO AVOID CONFUSION WITH YOUR CLIENTS.

Where will your work be used? Is the work going to be on billboards worldwide? Is it going to be used for a national campaign? Is it for a company's internal use?

Is it going to be printed? Is it going to be used for social media or on products?

How many rounds of rough sketches will you need to make? (It's usually three, but it depends on the project.)

Is the client going to re-use the art later?

How long are you going to work on the project?

What value do you put into your work?

If you look online, many artists don't mention their price range because it depends on the client and the project. Over time and with experience, you'll learn what fee to ask for or price to charge. Sometimes, the client may agree without saying anything. Other times, they will let you know if your price exceeds their budget. From there, you can start negotiating until you feel confident that you're receiving the right amount of money for your work. Understanding the value of your art is a process.

Don't be discouraged if you lose a job because your price is considered too high. It's okay if you don't get every contract. Each project is different, and if your client really wants to work with you, usually you can manage to negotiate a price that works for you both.

When you're negotiating fees, think about all your expenses, including paying for a place to live, your bills, your workspace, your taxes, and the tools you need to grow your art. You have the power to set your own prices based on the lifestyle you want to achieve through your art.

RECEIPT

DATE

PENCIL......12
PAINT........50
PAPER......20

TOTAL......12
TAX......

TO DO:
- CONTACT CLIENTS FOR NOT PAYING ON TIME

CONTACT ACCOUNTANT FOR ANNUAL TAX

INCOME THIS YEAR

INVOICE

ARTIST INFO
TAX ID
ADDRESS
BANK INFO

COMPANY INFO
ADDRESS

SERVICE OR PRODUCT

DESCRIPTION   PRICE

TOTAL PRICE

√ % CE ON/AC
MC MR M− M+
7 8 9 ÷
4 5 6 X
1 2 3 −
0 . = +

TRAVEL
EVENTS
ACCOUNTING
MARKETING
SOFTWARE
MATERIALS
RENT
SPENDING

TALKS
BOOKS
COMMISSION
ADVERTISEMENTS
PAINTINGS
PUZZLES
POSTERS
REVENUES

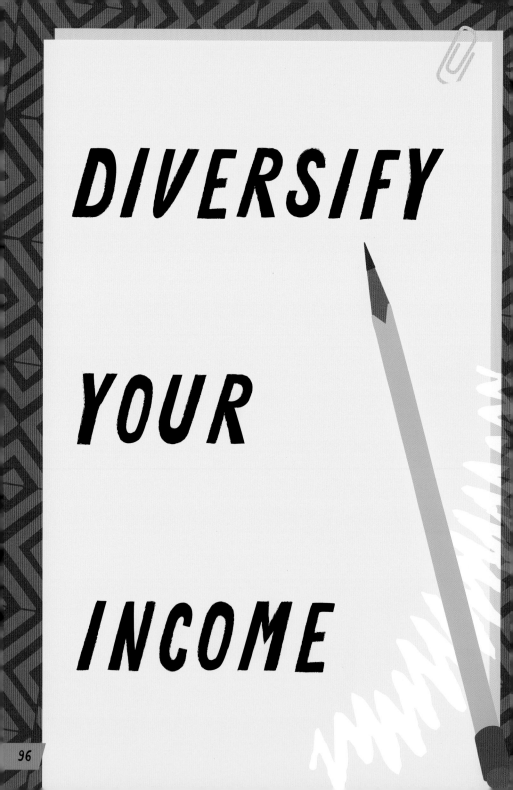

DIVERSIFY

YOUR

INCOME

As a creative, there are many ways of earning income. This is the money you earn or receive from the work you produce for a client. You don't always need to work more hours or weekends. So, how can you increase your income? Here are two ways:

Passive income for an illustrator is money you can earn without working on it all the time. Once set up, you won't have to spend too much time on it every day. Some passive income ideas may need some time, money, or effort at the beginning and you might need to check in on it sometimes, but it won't take up many hours each week.

Active income is money you earn by doing specific tasks or jobs within a set time. Examples include salaries, tips, fees, and commissions.

You can choose to focus on either or both of these ways of earning income. Just do what you feel comfortable with. It's good to start with general guidelines and then add your own unique approach to your business strategy.

PASSIVE INCOME

LICENCING

ONLINE COURSES

SERVICES

PRODUCTS

ACTIVE INCOME

COMMISSIONS

ADVANCES FOR BOOKS

PAINTINGS

ADVERTISEMENTS

CONFERENCES

EVENTS

Unlike a regular job, being freelance or self-employed means accepting that sometimes, you might not have lots of work. But at other times, you might have too much to do. It's important to manage your finances wisely. Saving money during busy periods means you can feel comfortable turning down jobs when you're already busy, and you're financially prepared for times when there are fewer jobs available.

WHAT ARE THE SERVICES YOU CAN PROVIDE AS A FREELANCE CREATIVE?

Editorial: Creating artwork for magazines, newspapers, or books.

Brand campaigns: Designing for brand advertisements.

Murals: Painting artwork on walls.

Animation: Creating animated artwork.

Painting: Selling your painted artwork.

Most illustrators rely on commissions and selling products, like posters. Relying solely on commissions can be challenging, because as soon as a project ends, finding new clients becomes necessary.

Diversifying your income sources allows for more flexibility and peace of mind, and gives you time for yourself.

PASSIVE INCOME

Passive incomes can save you time only when you already have a substantial following.

WHAT TYPE OF WORK WILL GIVE YOU A PASSIVE INCOME?

Licensing images: Selling your artwork on a design marketplace with a fee paid to you every time it is bought.

Masterclasses: Sharing your skills through PDFs or videos.

Online courses: Offering classes or workshops online.

Online shop: Having your own store where you promote and sell your products.

Independent shop: Running your own shop where you handle everything from production to shipping. It can be demanding but the good thing is you have full control and won't share your income with anyone else.

WHAT ABOUT ART MARKETS AND FAIRS?

Art markets are a great place to show your work to a new audience and get feedback. Look out for local markets or art fairs that might be happening near you. Remember, some markets require applications in advance, and you will likely need to pay for your spot at the market.

What can you sell at markets? Posters, cards, tote bags, key rings, stickers, puzzles, books, t-shirts, and more.

Exercise

How to build your business

Use a spreadsheet to create a file with all the months of the year. Make a list of the money you expect to earn from your active work and passive income for each month. You can set a goal for how much money you want to earn in a year. Look at the months where you have fewer jobs and focus on ways to earn more money through your passive income. You could achieve this by creating posters and cards, organizing an event, or selling your products at a market.

What prices should you set for your products?
Think about the following:

- Costs of production

- Packaging and posting

- The value of your work (time and creativity)

- If you're selling at a market, the cost of a table at the market and your time spent there

WHEN PROJECTS DON'T WORK OUT

As artists, we tend to take things personally when things don't work out, because our art is so intimate and linked to us. But it's important to distance ourselves a little when it comes to business, because the decisions a client makes go beyond us. Sometimes they have difficulties within their team and have to cancel or postpone the work. It's nothing against you personally, and maybe later when they fix their internal problems, they will get back to you.

All entrepreneurs fail before rising up and succeeding. That's why not everybody can work independently, as it's in the hard times that many people stop believing in themselves and give up. When something doesn't work out, it isn't a failure. It's actually a good way to learn and make your work better for next time.

BEING REPRESENTED BY AN AGENT

WHAT IS AN ILLUSTRATION AGENT?

Illustration agents guide illustrators and take care of the business side of things, like negotiating work fees with a client. They also help with contracts and make sure the illustrator gets paid on time. This means the illustrator can focus on the creative work.

Agents are good communicators and have an extensive network of clients, which means they can pitch the work of an illustrator to get them more jobs.

You don't have to have an agent, and when you are first starting out, I advise you to establish your own work first. Once you have proved you can get jobs, agents will come to you.

Although an agency may take care of a lot of the business side of your work, you still need to treat your work like a business. Keep track of your finances, contracts, and projects yourself.

WORKING WITH AN AGENT

Agents can't be your saviors and they won't make you a big star overnight. Signing with an agent isn't a magic solution that will magically increase your income.

Agents will promote your work to the best of their ability, but it doesn't mean you will get regular work straight away. Changing trends can make it difficult to guarantee jobs.

DON'T FORGET THAT YOU CREATE A RELATIONSHIP WITH YOUR AGENT, SO BE PROFESSIONAL AND MEET YOUR DEADLINES.

Before signing with an agent and the agency, I recommend you ask other artists working with the agency about their experience. Make sure you sign with someone who is interested in your whole career and understands which projects would be right for you.

Make sure you and your agent have a good working relationship. Commit to jobs and be professional with them. But remember to make sure you focus on your own business and growth too.

There are different types of contracts that artists can have with illustration agents. Some agents may require exclusive contracts, which means the artist can only work with that agent and not with any other agents. Some agents may have more flexible contracts that allow the artist to work with multiple agents or have more freedom in their professional choices. Some artists have agents in a different part of the world. For example, my illustration agency is based in New York and only operates in the USA and the UK.

Agents often work with artists with unique styles. They want to ensure that the artists don't feel like they're competing with other artists at the agency.

The thing to remember about an agent is that they will usually take a percentage of your earnings as a fee for representing you.

CONTRACT
BETWEEN
CLIENT
AND
ARTIST

REVIEW CONTRACT

SIGNATURE

CONTRACTS

When you work on a commissioned artwork, it's important to have a contract. This helps the client and the artist agree on terms and key details, which should help avoid complications later on. A contract should always be in writing.

HOW IS A CONTRACT STRUCTURED?

A contract has different parts to it, and it can be simple or more complex, depending on the project. Take your time to read and understand each section of a contract before signing, and seek professional guidance if you need to.

SOME THINGS TO THINK ABOUT

- Are the fees clearly detailed?

- When and how will you be paid?

- Are the dates when you're expected to deliver your artwork realistic? Is there enough time for you to do the work required?

- Are there deadlines along the way?

- Is what you're being asked to do clear?

- What credits will be you be given?

- Can you terminate the agreement, and what happens if you do?

- For longer or higher-priced jobs, is there a cancellation fee?

IN SHORT

Becoming a full-time artist IS possible by developing a brand and a communication strategy online. This includes having a website and social media channels to connect with a community of potential buyers and clients.

As an independent artist, it's smart to have multiple sources of income to navigate through uncertain periods.

The beauty of this job is that you are the one who builds the business in a way that suits you! You craft your business from A to Z. Just remember to stay consistent and focused, because running a business comes with lots of responsibilities. If you need help, you can reach out to an agent or seek legal advice.

The following are artists from around the world whom I have personally reached out to. As you will see in the following pages, there isn't just one path to becoming an artist, and nothing is set in stone. You have the freedom to take the time you need to pursue an artistic journey. Get ready to meet my friends!

TIM SINGLETON

www.timsingleton.rocks
www.instagram.com/timpsingleton

Tim studied Graphic Design in Toronto at OCAD University before becoming a full-time graphic designer.

As well as his full-time work, Tim also works freelance on various creative projects as an illustrator and designer. He collaborates with international brands and local organizations, often with a focus on the queer community.

Tim lives in Toronto, Canada, and he is a graphic designer, artist, and illustrator. He has worked for many companies and brands, including Starbucks, HuffPost, and YouTube. His artwork is bright, bold, and colorful. He draws his inspiration from pop culture, expressionism, pop art, abstract art, queer culture, and nature.

At a very young age, Tim knew that he wanted to be a creative, and at one point dreamed of becoming a Disney animator. Tim was inspired to pursue a creative journey by his older brother who was studying design at university.

AMRITA MARINO

www.amritamarino.com
www.instagram.com/amritamarino

Born in Kolkata, India, Amrita is an Indian-American illustrator living in the United States. Her artwork is filled with optimism, blending organic and dynamic lines to create a sense of tension and energy. She has worked with *The New York Times*, Amazon, Penguin Random House, and many more brands.

Amrita comes from a family with a strong engineering background, so, in the 1990s she pursued electrical engineering at a university in Kolkata. Once she obtained her degree, she left home and began working as an electrical engineer. When Amrita met an American man and fell in love, she moved to the US with him.

It was when she was in her 30s that Amrita changed her career direction and decided to study graphic design at the School of Visual Arts in New York City. Amrita's love for art was sparked by her

mom. When she was younger, the family home had stacks of colorful interior design magazines. Amrita would flip through the pages, soaking in the stunning pictures and imaginative designs and be inspired.

After studying, Amrita worked as a junior designer for Dwell Media where she designed and art-directed magazines. She frequently collaborated with illustrators and photographers on editorial projects.

A couple of years later, she became a freelance illustrator. Amrita didn't have a portfolio to showcase her work, but that didn't stop her. Through commissioned projects, she explored different artistic styles and discovered her own unique approach. When she faced moments of self-doubt, she listened to podcasts for inspiration. She says: "If you want to do something, do it without backup plans."

GEMMA O'BRIEN

Gemma is an Australian multidisciplinary artist who creates big and small paintings. Her work is centered around lettering and calligraphy, and inspired by Australian nature. She enjoys working for commercial clients and galleries.

Gemma studied law for a year before realizing she wanted to draw. She then studied communication design at university for four years.

Shortly after finishing her degree, Gemma began an internship at a visual effects company based in Sydney. There, she worked in the graphic design department and was offered a full-time job. When the company Gemma worked for closed, she faced a choice: should she become a freelancer or find a new job? Luckily, she had been in touch with an illustration agent who helped her overcome her insecurities and fears about freelancing. With their guidance and support, she made the decision to venture into independent work.

www.gemmaobrien.com
www.instagram.com/mrseaves101

114

provided Gemma with valuable opportunities to gain recognition and get major professional collaborations.

Gemma has been working as an artist for almost 10 years now and often travels to host workshops or talk about her experience as an independent artist, inspiring others along the way.

While Gemma was building her freelance career, she also took a job at a flower market. She posted her artwork on Instagram regularly and, thanks to the community she built up, her freelance career began to take off. At first, she faced challenges in managing everything as an entrepreneur. She made some mistakes, but her agent guided her in negotiating contracts and managing budgets with clients. Gemma's art has evolved over the years, allowing her to find her own unique artistic style.

Over time, more and more global brands wanted to work with her, so she left her Australian agent and took on joint agents based in the US and the UK. "Each continent has its own market and specificity," she says. Working for numerous US-based companies

ANDREA PIPPINS

Andrea is an African American author and freelance illustrator living in Sweden. Her visuals reflect the joy of being Black and proud. She has worked for brands and companies including Sephora, Malala Fund, and ESPN.

After obtaining her degree in Fine Arts from the Tyler School of Art and Architecture in the US, Andrea started her career as a junior designer at Hallmark Cards in Kansas City. She then moved to New York and worked as a graphic designer for three years. Later, she decided to pursue a post-graduate degree. After completing her masters in graphic design, she gained valuable experience as an assistant professor at several universities.

In 2013, an old colleague contacted her about an open position as a senior art director. Although she declined the job offer, she began to ask herself about who she was as an artist. She sought the guidance of a life coach and, in 2015, she resigned from her position as a professor and embarked on her freelance creative journey.

At an event called "Ladies Drawing Night," Andrea met an editor from Penguin Random House. Some months later, she shared her book ideas, including a coloring book called *I Love*

My Hair. Two weeks later, she got a book deal, and her journey as an author and children's book illustrator began.

Andrea has always documented her creative process on her blog and built a supportive community by sharing tips and inspiration. Since she was a child, she has always enjoyed both writing and illustrating. Today, she continues to engage with her audience through a newsletter, addressing topics that are close to her heart.

www.andreapippins.com
www.flygirlblog.com
www.instagram.com/andreapippins

HUSTON WILSON

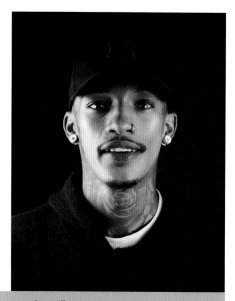

Huston is a graphic and lettering artist living in Johannesburg, South Africa. His work is colorful and uses letters to inspire. He creates bold, significant, and impactful letters. He has worked for various brands, including Amazon, Facebook, and Forbes.

At 16, he left school and began working to support his family as his father had left home. Huston's family has always supported him in pursuing an artistic path, even if it was not the typical path. They could see his passion when he was creating.

Huston's first daughter was born when he was 18, meaning he needed to find a stable and steady job. He held various day jobs, but in 2013, he wanted to change his creative journey. It was then that he discovered his passion for lettering design. Through the art of words, he found a way to express his deepest thoughts and emotions, bringing meaning to his creative practice. His mission became clear: inspire others with uplifting quotes and spread positive emotions to the world.

Huston found a job at his local church where he began making visuals for its events. He developed his style and taught himself graphic design and started composing images with lettering. This experience helped him to build a portfolio and led him to apply for a job as an art director.

In 2011, he became a freelance artist and participated in the *36 Days of Type* challenge via Instagram to explore and define his style. This pushed him to make more art and understand his style. He shared his artwork on Instagram, and to his delight, it quickly became popular and went viral.

Today, an agent at The Different Folk Agency represents Huston, and has helped him find jobs working on book covers and international brand campaigns. In 2021, he signed an extensive work campaign with Amazon where he has been able to explore different art mediums, such as animation and photography.

DDB is a place to grow personally as well as professionally.
If we bring our whole selves to work, and combine our unique perspectives and passions,
we will make each other more interesting. We'll enjoy the space for personal fulfillment, laughter, joy and celebration.
And it will show in the things we make.

DANIEL RAMIREZ PÉREZ

www.danielramirezperez.com
www.instagram.com/daniel.ramirez.perez

Daniel is a freelance illustrator who has worked with Sephora, Samsung, the *Financial Times*, and many other brands. Driven by vibrant colors and intricate geometrical shapes, his work radiates positive energy while celebrating the diversity of people in the world.

At 12 years old, Daniel knew he wanted to work in the art industry. He studied Fashion Design for four years in Munich, where he loved making fashion projects and sketching ideas. He worked at the *atelier* (workshop) of fashion brand Vivienne Westwood in London. There, he soon realized he didn't want to pursue fashion design.

So Daniel found a job as an art director at a design agency in Berlin where he connected with many talented illustrators. Inspired by their work, he decided to become an illustrator too. He sent his portfolio out to lots of companies, and a couple of months later, he got his first freelance job: creating a cover for the magazine, *L'Officiel Germany*.

Daniel started freelancing in his spare time while working a full-time job. Eventually, he gained a US agent and took the leap to become a full-time freelancer in 2018. Today, he lives in Berlin where he continues to pursue his passion successfully.

SONAKSHA

www.sonaksha.com
www.instagram.com/sonaksha

Sonaksha is a freelance writer, graphic designer, and illustrator living in Bangalore, India. Their artwork focuses on body image, gender, and important social issues like disability justice, mental health, and intersectional feminism.

They studied communication at university and received a general education in writing, filmmaking, and design. While studying, they took basic design classes in illustration and freelance writing, and contributed to blogs and newspapers.

Sonaksha switched from writing to illustrating, following their passion for drawing. In India, where art schools were scarce and expensive, it wasn't a common career choice. But they defied the odds and pursued their artistic dreams.

Sonaksha is not represented by an agent and manages everything independently. They learned by making mistakes, but their previous experiences as a freelance writer helped them to manage the financial and administrative aspects of being a freelance illustrator today.

Sonaksha improved their illustration skills and shared their work on social media to connect with other people facing health challenges. As a freelancer, they have found solace in the online community, especially as a queer person in India. Sonaksha's illustrations raise awareness of important issues. During the pandemic, their work on a post on how to help Mutual Aid India went viral.

TEMI COKER

www.temicoker.co
www.instagram.com/temi.coker

traditional path, so he studied biomedical engineering when he moved to the US. He tried to make his parents proud, but he couldn't continue because, deep down, he was creative. So he began a degree in digital media, where he studied photography and graphic design. While studying, he worked for a church to create flyers and sermon series while also doing photography on the side. Working in the creative industry during and after college prepared him for the world of work. He learned how to value his work and deal with clients when it came to negotiating deals.

For Temi Coker, Black is a beautiful canvas. He sees Black people as strong and joyful and aims to show the African diaspora through his work. His work is colorful and a mix between graphic design and photography.

Temi was born in Nigeria. When he was younger, he wanted to be a musician, but his family preferred that he follow a more

BLACK & BEAUTIFUL

programme, he made many new work contacts and was given jobs. In the beginning, he found it hard to know how much to charge clients for his work. He first learned by making mistakes in negotiating before he got an agent at ATRBUTE in New York with whom he has a great relationship.

Today, Temi wants to create more personal projects that fuel his creativity, including ventures like prints, tote bags, and jackets that can generate passive income. He wants to turn his love for posters into wearable art and is excited for the journey ahead.

At 22 years old, Temi became a teacher. At the same time, he embarked on a personal project—creating a daily poster—to explore new avenues of artistic expression.

After three years of teaching, Temi applied for the Adobe Creative Residency 2018. He was accepted for the year-long program and was paid to keep creating his daily posters. This opportunity allowed him to delve even deeper into his creative journey and push the boundaries of his artistic expression. He decided to make posters for the sports, music, and fashion industries.

After the residency, Temi saved money and worked hard to become an independent artist. Thanks to this

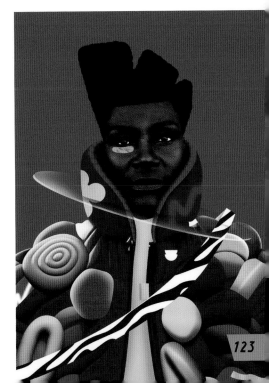

JESSICA WALSH

At 11 years old, Jessica Walsh taught herself how to code and design websites. She then created an HTML site to teach other children how to make websites. Since she was very young, she has always dreamed of having her own art studio. Her success early on with web design gave her the confidence to attend art school and dedicate her life to design.

Jessica went to the Rhode Island School of Design, where she took introductory courses in drawing, painting, ceramics, photography, and woodworking. Coming from a digital background, this was all new and exciting. In her second year, she focused on graphic design and learned how to combine art and handmade elements with her digital skills. Her work today is influenced by handmade art and craft mixing with design and photography.

Jessica's mom was a strong role model, showing her that anything is possible with hard work, time, and persistence. When Jessica was growing up, her parents started their own business with no money or family support. They built it into something meaningful and profitable, and seeing their tireless hard work has helped to shape Jessica's work ethic.

Jessica's artistic style reflects her personality, inspirations, memories, and experiences. Jessica's style developed when she started working for a print

magazine in 2008. The economy had crashed and the magazine's budgets for illustration and photography were small, so she taught herself photography and set design to start creating cover and interior artwork for the magazine.

Jessica discovered her unique style of colorful handcrafted set design, and tried techniques such as body painting and creating graphic bodysuits. Inspired by her love of challenges, she decided to start her own design and branding agency—called "And Walsh"—to work with new clients.

Realizing the importance of joy and avoiding burnout, she made space for passion projects alongside client work. Surprisingly, she found that working on personal projects made her even more enthusiastic and productive with her client work. It turned out that following her passions made her work faster and better. Her personal work also attracted new clients. These projects included work for Ladies, Wine & Design, 12 Kinds of Kindness, Pins Won't Save the World, 40 Days of Dating, and Let's Talk About Mental Health.

Jessica loves working on graphic design and photography projects that make a positive impact on social movements, culture, and the design community.

NDUBISI OKOYE

www.instagram.com/n_du_time
www.ndubisiokoye.com

When Ndubisi was younger, he wanted to be an athlete. Unfortunately, he wasn't able to get a sports scholarship, so he focused on art instead. He chose to study graphic design and learned skills such as silk-screen printing, digital graphic design, and classic art. His family supported him to follow a creative career, and that helped him to stay focused and achieve his dreams. Many events led him to where he is now, and he says, "You don't become an artist. You remember you are one."

Before he'd even graduated from the College for Creative Studies in Detroit with a degree in advertising design, Ndubisi was working as an art director at advertising agencies.

Ndubisi Okoye is a multidisciplinary creative and creative director. He makes vibrant, hand-lettered visuals with geometric shapes, and draws bold portraits and tribal patterns. Through his works, he wants to show the power and beauty of Blackness. Over time, his art style has changed. He started by drawing famous people in black and white, but eventually began incorporating vibrant colors into his work. Through his art, Ndubisi expresses a more extroverted side of himself, which is a contrast to his introverted nature.

Besides his current job as a senior art director, Ndubisi works on various personal projects, such as vibrant mural paintings, custom hand lettering, and thought-provoking illustrations. His clients include Universal Music Group, Pepsi, Netflix, Warner Bros., Adobe, and The LEGO® Group.

Editors Vicky Armstrong and Harriet Birkinshaw
Project Art Editor Chris Gould
Designer Samantha Richiardi
Project Picture Researcher Rituraj Singh
Senior Production Editor Marc Staples
Senior Production Controller Louise Minihane
Senior Acquisitions Editor Katy Flint
Managing Art Editor Vicky Short
Publishing Director Mark Searle

DK would like to thank Sarah Harland for proofreading
and Alastair Dougall for editorial assistance.

First American Edition, 2023
Published in the United States by DK Publishing
1745 Broadway, 20th Floor, New York, NY 10019

A catalog record for this book
is available from the Library of Congress.
ISBN: 978-0-7440-8963-9

DK books are available at special discounts when purchased
in bulk for sales promotions, premiums, fund-raising,
or educational use. For details, contact:
DK Publishing Special Markets,
1745 Broadway, 20th Floor, New York, NY 10019
SpecailSales@dk.com

Printed and bound in China

The publisher would like to thank the following for their kind permission to reproduce their photographs:
(Key: a-above; b-below/bottom; c-center; f-far; l-left; r-right; t-top)

112 Tim Singleton. **113** Amrita Marino. **114-115** Gemma O'Brien. **114** Gemma O'Brien: Jeremy Shaw (tr).
116 Andrea Pippins: (cra). **117** Andrea Pippins: An illustration for AWID's Movements Matter project
highlighting human rights, equality and justice (cr); Commissioned artwork for Bloomberg in celebration
of Black History Month (tl); We Inspire Me, A collection of tips and advice on how to create and nurture
one's creative community (tr); Spread from Becoming Me, a resource to encourage young readers to live
a creative life (cl). **118** Hust Wilson: (cla); APRIL- Personal Project for Hust Wilson (br). **119** Hust Wilson:
DDB (Doyle Dane Bernbach)- Freedom to be (b); Forbes Spain- 75 mejores empresas para trabajar
(75 best companies to work for) (cra). **120** Daniel Ramirez Perez: (ca). **121** Sonaksha: (br); Mutual Aid India,
2021, Sonaksha (cla). **122-123** Temi Coker. **124-125** Creative Agency/Design Studio: &Walsh.
126-127 Ndubisi okoye: Techtown, LEGO and Universal Music Group